018 Chores

	1	2	3	4	5	6	7	8	9	10	11	12
ash/change sheets	X											
ash/change towels												
lean tub												
ean toilet												
ust												
ipe appliances												
lean out fridge												
rub stove												
ust blinds/windows												
ash duvets	X											
vash couch												
lean mirrors												
lean baseboards												
rganize/clean pantry												
rganize closets												
otate toys/clothes												

INDEX